The Word of the Rose

Dale Stubbart

The Word of the Rose

Word

Perhaps the first word we think of when we hear the word *Rose* is the word *Love*. Roses are considered to be an intimate gift by some.

Most of us are familiar with Roses. Most have seen a Rose, held it, and deeply inhaled its fragrance – though the fragrance causes headaches for some.

But just how familiar are we with the Rose? How intimate are we with it?

In this book, I'll explore the various parts of the Rose in more detail without getting technical.

Many things in this book you'll already be familiar with. I hope you enjoy the memories.

If you're looking to give an intimate gift like a Rose, perhaps it will make it a more special gift if you're more intimate with it.

Every species has their own language. This is the Word of the Rose.

I hope you read it with a Rosy disposition.

The Word of the Rose

Rose

A Rose by any other name, is still the cutest flower in the whole petunia patch!

Rose brings to mind the flower, we often forget the Thorns.

Rose is also a Color – a dark pink to moderate red.

Rose is also a perforated nozzle for spraying or sprinkling water, used for watering, among other things – Roses.

A Rose is a gem cut, a Rose window, and a compass card.

When something is Roses, or comes up Roses, it is marked by favor, success, or ease of execution.

You'd almost think Rose was a suit of cards, like diamonds or hearts.

The Word of the Rose

A Rosette is a decorative knot. And a very fancy knot was untied when the Rosetta stone was translated.

A ceiling Rose is a decorative base attached to the ceiling. Often this is the base of a light fixture.

Let us not forget the Tudor Rose or the Yellow Rose of Texas.

And last, but not least, let us not forget the words of Roger Miller:
"England swings like pendulum do
Bobbies on bicycle, two-by-two
Westminster Abbey, the tower of Big Ben
The Rosey red cheeks of the little children"

The Word of the Rose

Thorns

The Stem of the Rose has many Thorns, as anyone who's picked one up knows only all too well.

A Thorn is also any Thorny plant, usually referred to as a brier or bramble.

Thorn is the runic letter þ which is pronounced th.

The Thorn is the symbol of suffering, most often expressed by the saying, "He's a Thorn in my side". I'm not sure why the Thorn's in the side, I would have thought it would be a Thorn in my foot, or at least in my hand.

A Thorn is also called a prick, pricker, prickle, spinule, spine, sticker, and a barb.

When caught by a Thorn, it is then called a wait-a-minute.

Acantho- is the prefix for Thorn. Remember that next time you're working a crossword puzzle.

The Word of the Rose

Roses which have no Thorns are considered (biologically) unarmed. Roses, with or without Thorns, unarm us.

And as we leave the Thorn, remember the story of Androcles, who was spared by a lion in the arena, when the lion remembered that Androcles had once pulled a Thorn from the lion's paw.

I'll bet Androcles was trying very hard to jog that lion's memory!

The Word of the Rose

Stem

The Stem holds the other parts of the Rose together. Similarly in linguistics, the Stem is the main part of the word, to which the other parts are added. Thus, the Stem is the main part of the Rose. And here we thought it was the Flower.

For larger plants, the Stem is the stalk, or the trunk. In humans, the Stem is the torso; some of which are Rosy.

Stem can also be a verb meaning arise, derive, emanate, flow, issue, originate, proceed, rise, or spring.

In direct opposition, Stem can also mean to stop. When we are flooded by opposition, we must place a Rose in the stream and Stem the tide.

The Stem is that part of the Rose which supports it and holds it upright. Without the Stem, the Rose would just sit on the ground. However, the Rose would still look good.

The Latin for Stem is caulis. Just in case you were curious.

From head to foot, is from Stem to stern; although I've never heard of the front of a ship being referred to as the Stem.

Without the Stem, there would be no such thing as a long-Stemmed Rose. At the same time, a Rose with the Stem removed is a Stemmed Rose, it just ain't long!

The Word of the Rose

A Rose without its Stem is still beautiful. Our brain without a Stem might be beautiful, but it might cause us a wee problem or two!

The Word of the Rose

Leaves

The Leaves of the Rose use photosynthesis to create chlorophyll. They let the Rose breathe and feed it sugar.

The Leaves of this book are its pages. Leaf through it to let it breathe.

If I laminated the Leaves of this book with gold Leaf, the book would be worth more. It would also have a nice sheen.

A Leaf is sometimes called a frond, flag, blade, or foliole.

If there's not room on your table for a Rose, just add a Leaf. If it's a big Rose, add a frond.

Sometimes people say, "Leave me alone", but then they're sad if you make like a tree and Leave. And they'll be disappointed in your Leave of absence.

But if you've been with them in their rocky boat long enough, surely you deserve some shore Leave. After all, they said it was ok to Leave.

A Leaflet is a small handout, usually distributed by missionaries or politicians.

The Word of the Rose

By your Leave
Don't Leave me your riches
Don't Leave me your fame
But Leave me your love

And always remember, Leif Ericson may have discovered America, but Native Americans were already there.

The Word of the Rose

Flower

The Flower of the Rose is the most attractive part, as it is the Flower which attracts us so to the Rose.

Actually, it is the petals of the Flower which attract us to the Rose. The petals are actually a privacy screen separating us from seeing the reproductive processes at work.

As the Flower matures, it goes from bud to full Flower. A Rose given to a girl, will make you a bud for life.

Grains usually don't Flower, they just are turned to Flour.

The Flower is also called the bloom. And I'm sometimes called a bloomin' idiot. At other times, when I bloom, I'm in my prime.

A small Flower is a Floret. Roses don't fit this category, unless, perhaps they're wild or native Roses. Native Roses of the United States include the Prickly Rose, Prairie Rose, Smooth Rose, Pigmy Rose, California Wild Rose, White Prairie Rose, Little Woods Rose or Dwarf Rose, Mancos Rose, Ensenada Rose, Shining Rose, Swamp Rose, Alpine Rose or Mountain Rose, Cluster Rose, Climbing Rose or

The Word of the Rose

Illinois Rose, Ground Rose, Desert Rose, Woods Rose, and
Cascade Rose.

https://davesgarden.com/guides/articles/view/710

In the sixties we had Flower children, otherwise known
as hippies. Alas, the children now, are often more interested
in money than Flowers. Flower children may have faded
from the news, but most major newspapers carry a section
on growing Flowers; often called the Garden Section.

The prefix for Flower is antho-. The suffix is –florous.
So, anthoflorous would be Flower-Flower?

Flora is the goddess of Flowers.

If only we had more Florigen, the plant hormone which
promotes Flowering, we'd be in our prime more often. And
if we realized we were in our prime, we'd be less prone to
sit out the dance of life as wall-Flowers. I guess we'll just
have to look at the Rose and see if we can get some
Florigen by osmosis!

The Word of the Rose

Scent

Various Roses have various Scents. I think that all Roses are fragrant. But according to some, only a few of the more than 200 species of Rose have Scents.

The Damask Rose or the Rose of Castile, is usually sought out for Rose water, Rose oil, or Rose concrete – a waxy compound containing Rose Scent which is used in cosmetics.

The Gallic Rose, French Rose, or Rose of Provins species include the Apothecary Rose. The Scent of this Rose reminds us of being at the Pharmacist's.

The Provence Rose, Cabbage Rose, or Rose de Mai species has a clear, sweet Scent with a touch of honey. The Latin name is Rosa centifolia, meaning hundred-leaved Rose. Pliny and Theophrastus both mention a hundred-leaved Rose, but Rosa centifolia is a hybrid developed by the Dutch much later in the 1500's.

The Musk Rose is suspected to originally have come from the western Himalayas.

The Word of the Rose

Many believe the Bourbon Rose to have been developed by the French. It is hard to be sure, especially since Bourbon Rose oil comes from Bourbon Roses grown in India (and probably elsewhere). Bourbon Roses are said to smell like bourbon; or to have hints of raspberries and nectarines; or to have hints of incense, coffee, and balsam.

The China Rose species is native to China. The China Rose is said to contain a tea Scent.

The White Rose of York has a lighter more delicate floral aroma. The Scent of this Rose is usually referred to as Bulgarian White Rose.

The Word of the Rose

Roots

Roses also have roots – a long anchor root, and thinner, shorter fibrous ones. The Roots of course hold the Rose in the ground. By the time many of us see a Rose, the Roots are gone. We frequently only get to see a Rose from the Stem up.

A Root is also the basic cause, source, or origin of something. "The love of money is the Root of all evil." First Timothy 6:10

To Root means to establish deeply and firmly.

Pigs Root by pushing their snout into something repeatedly, sometimes for food, sometimes for comfort. Often what they root into is the ground.

A Root of unity is a complex number which is the nth root of one.

To solve an equation is to find its Root.

The Word of the Rose

Roots is the story and TV Series of a Gambian, who is sold into slavery, and his descendants for seven generations.

In music, the fundamental note of a chord is its Root.

In Chinese culture, the constellation Libra is the constellation Root.

The Word of the Rose

Color

As previously mentioned, Rose is also a Color – a dark pink to moderate red. Rose is the Color halfway between red and magenta. For webpages, this is the color FF007F or 255,0,128.

Variations on the Color Rose include Misty Rose, Tea Rose, Tickle Me Pink, Persian Pink, Rose Pink, Rose Bonbon, Brilliant Rose, Thulian Pink, Brink Pink, French Rose, Razzmatazz, Razzle Dazzle Rose, Persian Rose, Fuchsia Rose, Rose Red, Dogwood Rose, Raspberry Rose, China Rose, Rose Quartz, Rosy Brown, Old Rose, Rose Vale, Cordovan, Rose Taupe, Rose Ebony, and Rosewood.

Red Roses symbolize love.

Light Pink Roses symbolize the gift of grace.
Dark Pink Roses symbolize gratitude and appreciation.
Pink Roses also symbolize admiration, gentleness, gladness, and sweetness.

Peach Roses symbolize modesty. I assume this would include Apricot Roses. Peach Roses are a simple way to say *Thank you*.

The Word of the Rose

Orange Roses symbolize fascination, enthusiasm, desire, and excitement.

Salmon Roses also symbolize desire and excitement.

Yellow Roses can symbolize infidelity. Yellow Roses also symbolize the joy of friendship.

White Roses are for hearts new to love. They symbolize new beginnings, remembrance, and innocence.

Ivory or Cream (Off-White) Roses symbolize charm and thoughtfulness.

Purple Roses symbolize enchantment. I assume this would include Lavender Roses.

Burgundy Roses symbolize unconscious beauty. I assume this would include Mauve Roses.

Green Roses symbolize rejuvenation.
https://www.goodhousekeeping.com/holidays/valentines-day-ideas/g1352/rose-color-meanings/
http://www.passiongrowers.com/web/ot/colors.asp

You might also sometimes find multi-Colored and rainbow-hued Roses.

If you're giving the gift of Roses or any other flower for that matter, it might be good to include a note to ensure that the recipient is hearing the same language as the one you're speaking.

The Word of the Rose

Growing

I am not an expert at growing Roses. My grandmother on the other hand was quite the expert. She even invented a new variety of Rose and won some awards for Growing Roses.

When we moved into our house, we had six Rose plants growing in our back yard. They were more like trees than bushes, each being about four feet tall on a single stem. Since there is a lot of shade in our backyard, we moved them to the front yard near the street where they would receive the most light.

Little did we know that deer love Roses. Our back yard was fenced. Our front yard was not. The deer were not bothered by the Thorns. Or at least they were not bothered enough to quit eating the buds before they had fully blossomed. Eventually the Roses grew over 7 feet tall, and the deer quit eating them. We also planted other plants near them which quickly formed a wall around the Roses, keeping out even the deer.

We cleared out quite a bit of the dense undergrowth in that area the other day. When we were done, I noticed that one of the Roses was now 20 feet tall.

We also had Woods Rose, a native variety, already growing in the yard.

We had a Landscape Company, Patterns in Design, install a rain garden for us. They planted a Nootka Rose (another native variety) in the rain garden. There's a four-foot wide berm that we need to keep clear between our yard and the street. Every year, the Nootka Rose grows out into the street several times and has to be pruned back to keep it where it belongs.

Here are suggestions from the internet to help you grow Roses:

- Plant banana peels in the ground near them.
- Play music to them.
- Add alfalfa meal to their potting mixture.
- Place them where they'll get six hours of sun per day. Good luck with that here in the Pacific Northwest.
- Plant them in rich, well-draining soil. The Roses were doing just fine in our clay soil, especially the Woods Roses.
- Place organic mulch around them.
- Water them deeply. Not a problem with all the rain we get.
- Inspect them for insects and diseases.
- Prune them regularly. I guess they mean unless you want them to grow 20 feet tall.

https://www.bayeradvanced.com/articles/6-secrets-to-growing-roses

Let's see. I didn't plant banana peels – those go into my compost to feed the worms. My worms love banana peels, almost as much as they love shredded paper which is their favorite food.

I don't play music to them. Not unless you count all the birds singing to them. The birds came in mostly with the rain garden.

I didn't add any alfalfa meal or anything else. My wife may have added some azomite. And she may have added other nutrients when we transplanted them.

Between the shade and the rain, they're not getting much sun.

We have well-draining soil in the rain garden. The rest of our yard is mostly clay. There's also a layer about two feet underground of something so hard, that when rain reaches that level it comes back up to the surface. When the water returns to the surface, it bubbles and looks like a spring.

Organic mulch was not used on the Woods Roses. It was probably used when the tall Roses were transplanted. And it was probably used at first on the Nootka Rose.

The rain waters our Roses deeply. We may have watered the tall Roses deeply when they were transplanted.

We never inspect them. We're way too busy for that.

We prune them when they get out of control.

Seems to be working so far.

The Word of the Rose

Women

And now, let us celebrate some Women named Rose.

Rosa Parks was a black woman who lived during the civil rights movement in the US. She was famous for refusing to move to the back of a bus, so that a white man could sit in her seat. The white man was fully capable of moving to a seat in the back of the bus, but those were relegated to black people. Blacks were allowed to sit in the front, unless a white person asked them to move.

Roseanne Barr is an actress, best known for her TV Series Roseanne. She placed 6th in the 2012 Presidential race.

Rosie O'Donnell is an actress, best known for her TV Series, The Rosie O'Donnell Show.

Rose McGowan is an actress, best known for playing Paige Matthews in the TV Series Charmed.

Rosalynn Carter is the wife of US President Jimmy Carter. Along with President Carter, she co-founded the Carter Institute which tries to wage peace, fight disease, and build hope. She created the Carter Center Mental Health Task Force. She also is the president of the board of the Rosalynn Carter Institute for Caregiving.

Rose Kennedy was the mother of President John Kennedy, and of senators Robert and Ted Kennedy. She was given the title Countess for exemplary motherhood by Pope Pius XII.

Rosalie Ham is an Australian Author. She wrote The Dressmaker, Summer at Mount Hope, and There Should Be More Dancing.

Betty White played Rose Nylund on the TV Series The Golden Girls.

Rhoda (which is Rose in Greek) was the girl in the Bible who opened the door for Peter when he returned from jail to the congregation.

Rosemary Brown was the first black woman to be elected to office in Canada.

Rosina Bulwer Lytton wrote 14 novels including A Blighted Life which tells of her incarceration in a madhouse by her husband.

Rhoda Merganstern was Mary Richard's neighbor in the TV Series The Mary Tyler Moore Show and in Rhoda. Rhoda was played by Valerie Harper.

Rosalie is a musical by George Gershwin and Sigmund Romberg. It tells of a Princess who falls in love with a Lieutenant.

The Word of the Rose

Rosina Lawrence played Mary Roberts in Way Out West.

Rosalie Silberman Abella was the first Jewish woman to sit on the Canadian Supreme Court.

Rosina is courted by a Count in the Opera The Barber of Seville.

Rosie the Riveter was a representation of Women who worked in factories and shipyards during World War II.

St Rosalia is the Patron Saint of Palermo, Italy. She is also known as The Little Saint.

Roseanna McCoy is a main character in, and the name of, a movie about the feud between the Hatfields and the McCoys.

Rosanna is a song by the rock group Toto. The main lyrics are *Rosanna* and *Meet you all the way*.

Rosita is a five-year old Muppet on Sesame Street.

Rosetta LeNoire is best known for her role as Mother Winslow in the TV Show Family Matters.

Rosita Farisi is one of the companions of Doctor Who.

There are many other famous Women named Rose or one of its variants.

The Word of the Rose

Men

Similarly let's celebrate Men named Rose. Rosey is short for Roosevelt which means *field of Roses.*

Rosey Grier was a professional football player for the New York Giants and the Los Angeles Rams. He became an actor and played Gabe Cooper in the TV Series Daniel Boone. He also appeared in other TV shows. Rosey is also a singer and a minister. He was a bodyguard to Robert Kennedy.

Rosey Brown was a professional football player for the New York Giants.

Rosy Roosevelt was an American diplomat and brother of President Franklin Roosevelt.

The Word of the Rose

Places

Let's also celebrate Places named Rose.

"Match me such marvel save in Eastern clime
A Rose-Red city – half as old as time!"
John William Burgon describing Petra, Jordan.

Marrakech, Morocco is called the Rose City in reference to all its Rose-colored buildings.

Portland, Oregon is nicknamed The Rose City for all its Rose gardens.

Rosario is the third most populous city in Argentina.

985 Rosina is an asteroid, as is 540 Rosamunde.

Rose Island is a small island in the Bahamas. There are four Rose Islands in Canada, another in Rhode Island, another in Germany, and yet another in New Zealand. There's a Rose Isle in the UK, and a Rose Atoll in American Samoa.

The Word of the Rose

Bouquet

Now let us tie this collection of Roses into a pretty Bouquet.

The Holy Rosary is a form of prayer in the Catholic Church. The Rosary also refers to a string of beads or knots used to count the prayers. Rosary means crown or garland or Roses. These prayers recall events in the lives of Jesus and Mary his mother.

The Rosetta Stone is a stone which had a decree inscribed in it. The decree was inscribed three times, once in ancient Greek, the other two times in two different Egyptian scripts. The Rosetta Stone was the key to deciphering Egyptian Hieroglyphs.
Rosetta Stone is a language learning software.

The Pink Rose is a Filipino butterfly.

Black Rose is a grape.

Rosa Blanca (White Rose) is a political party in Italy.

The Word of the Rose

The Yellow Rose of Texas is an American folksong. It was sung by several people including Elvis Presley and Willie Nelson.

Yellow Roses was a number one hit song by Dolly Parton.

Rational Rose is a software tool by IBM for visual modeling and construction of application modules.

Rosy is a computer app for use by salons and spas.

Rosé is a pink wine. Sometimes it is a mix of red and white wines.

Rosemary is an Italian herb of the mint family.

And on that fragrant note, The Word of the Rose concludes.